THE RED·LIGHT Ladies OF VIRGINIA·CITY NEVADA

BY GEORGE WILLIAMS III

The Redlight Ladies of Virginia City, Nevada
by George Williams III

6th printing March, 1990
Published by:
Tree By The River Publishing
P.O. Box 935
Dayton, Nevada 89403

Other related books by George Williams III:
Rosa May: The Search For A Mining Camp Legend
Mark Twain: His Life In Virginia City, Nevada
Mark Twain: His Adventures At Aurora And Mono Lake
Mark Twain: Jackass Hill and the Jumping Frog
The Guide to Bodie and Eastern Sierra Historic Sites
The Murders At Convict Lake
Hot Springs of the Eastern Sierra

Library of Congress Cataloging in Publication Data

Williams, George III.
        The redlight ladies of Virginia City, Nevada.
Summary: Discusses prostitution in Virginia City, Nevada in the late nineteenth century and profiles the lives of several prostitutes and madams.
    1.Prostitution—Nevada—Virginia City—History—19th century. [1. Prostitution—Nevada—Virginia City—History. 2. Prostitutes] I.Title.
HQ 146.V55W55   1984   306.7'42'0979356   84-147
ISBN 0-935174-13-3
ISBN 0-935174-12-5 (pbk.)

Printed in the United States of America

Author's Introduction

Between 1860-82, Virginia City, Nevada, was the largest, richest mining town in the American West. Virginia City's silver mines produced 293 million dollars during the boom years and an additional 55 million dollars from 1883-1919.

Virginia City was comprised mostly of single men, a ratio of men to women as high as 8 to 1, never less than 3 to 1. The lack of affordable housing, the hostile environment, the high cost of travel, and the expense of living in Virginia City prevented many men from bringing their wives, girl friends and families to Virginia City. Hoards of prostitutes and madams came to Virginia City to capitalize on the lack of women.

Prostitution was lawfully permitted in Virginia City from 1859 until 1947 when it was outlawed. During these years, hundreds of prostitutes and madams made their livings and died within the Virginia City redlight districts. This book tells of their lives, deaths and legends based on newspaper accounts, Federal, State and Storey County records.

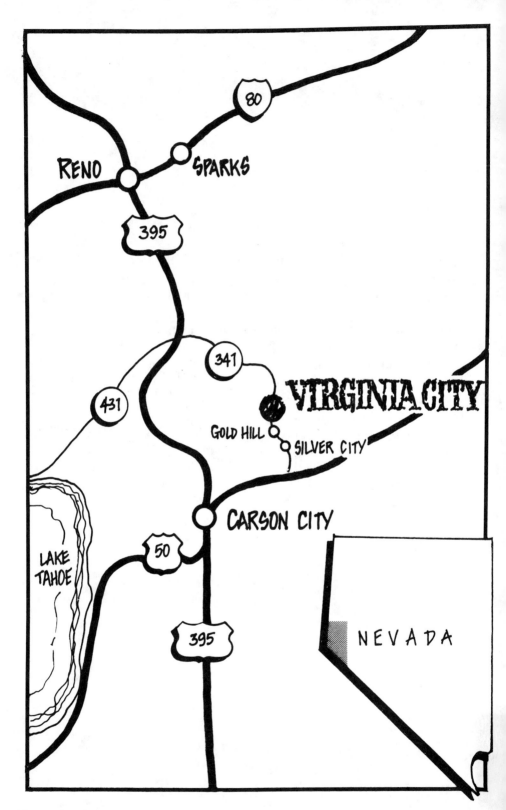

The Redlight Districts

Virginia City had three redlight districts. The primary redlight district was on the West side of D Street in the five block area from Washington Street, north to Mill Street. Most, but certainly not all, the redlight women worked here. There were scattered houses of prostitution, some on E Street, some even as high up as the B Street residential district.

The D Street redlight district was located behind many of the most popular C Street saloons. Backstairs led down from the saloons to the heart of the redlight. The D Street redlight was also directly across the street from the Virginia and Truckee depot. The train literally dumped arriving passengers into the redlight district. Citizens leaving town were forced to pass through the redlight to reach the depot.

The district was located as near to the major mines as possible. Hundreds of miners passed through the redlight district going to and coming from work. The temptation of a few pleasurable moments was flaunted before the miners daily and nightly.

The primary redlight district was highly visible to all who came to or lived in Virginia City. This high visibility helped the D Street redlight district to be extraordinarily profitable for landlords, madams and prostitutes.

The secondary redlight district, known as the Barbary Coast, was on Virginia City's main thoroughfare, C Street, where the bulk of the town's businesses were located. The Barbary Coast was located on the west side of C Street in the one block area from Silver Street north to Flowery. The name Barbary Coast was likely taken from San Francisco's infamous Barbary Coast district, a sordid collection of dives, whorehouses and cow yards — large hotels which at times housed several hundred lower class prostitutes who sold their services for as low as two-bits, a quarter. Virginia City's Barbary Coast was a small collection of saloon-brothels where men could meet and drink with lower class prostitutes — most unattractive — and have sex with them in backrooms. The most well known places were Mr. and Mrs. Corcoran's at 158 South C, Nellie Sayer's at 146½ South C, Peter Larkin's at 146 South C and Pat Gould's. A Virginia City journalist described these places as, "gin shops of the lowest class... buildings are low one story doggeries, with an appearance such as to warn most people the nature of their occupants. The front part of both are barrooms, the back part are bedrooms."

In 1877 there was a crackdown on the Barbary Coast dives. A journalist wrote:

> There are a few dives on the Barbary Coast which should be removed or suppressed. The only, or about the only, means of reaching the new 4th ward school house, where the high school is taught, is along C Street and past these dives of sin. There prostitution flaunts its gay colors and there the coarse jest, the vulgar oath and the filthiest of conversation is heard at all hours of the day and night. It is time something was done to put a

stop to all this, as now carried on on the principal street of our city, along which our girls, just blooming into maidenhood are compelled to pass and repass.

An 1877 cleanup campaign closed all the Barbary Coast saloon-brothels. However, some reopened several years later.

The third redlight district was in Chinatown at the far northeast corner of the city near the cemetery. Here Chinese girls and young women, either bought from their parents or stolen, were enslaved and forced into lives of prostitution. In 1875 there were 75 Chinese prostitutes in 1880, 20.

No photographs exist of the Virginia City D Street redlight district, as it looked in the 1860's. Over the years the district changed much due to the flimsy structure of the buildings, fires caused by lunatic incendiaries, faulty stoves and stove pipes. The entire D Street redlight was completely destroyed by fire in 1871 and 1875. After each fire the district was hastily rebuilt.

During the early 1860's, prostitutes hung blue lanterns outside their doors to attract customers. In time, houses of prostitution became well known.

Prostitution was always legal in Virginia City during the early mining days. However, the Board of Alderman and leading men of the town preferred prostitution be confined to the three block area on D Street. An 1878 ordinance attempted to set boundaries for the district but these boundaries were largely ignored. Houses of prostitution were allowed to operate outside the D Street district — even in the residential B Street area. However, if a house became too noisy, violent, or if its occupants got on the bad side of police, the houses were usually closed and the operators and prostitutes arrested. Operators were charged with running a "disorderly house" and penalized small fines. Sometimes they were asked to leave town as was Nellie Sayers who ran a dive saloon-brothel on the Barbary Coast.

Virginia City prostitutes were not licensed as were prostitutes in some American cities. Nor were houses of prostitution licensed or taxed. Operators were usually forced to pay high rents to landlords and to pay off police and elected officials. Policemen nearly always were allowed "freebies" in exchange for non-harrassment.

The D Street redlight district was comprised of other respectable businesses. There were saloons, dance houses, and bawdy theaters such as the Alhambra Theater in the basement of the Frederick House on the northwest corner of D and Union Streets. There were bakeries, print shops, melodeons, livery stables, hotels, lodging houses, City Hall for a time and the police station. Most men considered houses of prostitution another form of business and tolerated them.

Though prostitution was allowed, prostitutes were sometimes arrested for soliciting prostitution. The 1878 ordinance by the Board of Alderman, prohibited women from soliciting prostitution by exhibiting themselves in doorways, through windows, on street corners, calling to passersby, etc. as they had done in the past. A temporary crackdown by Officer Jim Breen quieted the

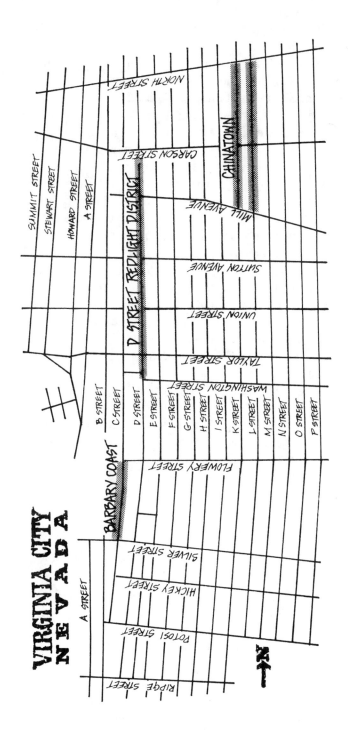

VIRGINIA CITY
NEVADA

A STREET

RIDGE STREET

POTOSI STREET

HICKEY STREET

SILVER STREET

N

BARBARY COAST

FLOWERY STREET

B STREET
C STREET
D STREET
E STREET
F STREET
G STREET
H STREET
I STREET
K STREET
L STREET
M STREET
N STREET
O STREET
P STREET

WASHINGTON STREET

TAYLOR STREET

UNION STREET

SUTTON AVENUE

MILL AVENUE

CARSON STREET

NORTH STREET

D STREET REDLIGHT DISTRICT

CHINATOWN

SUMMIT STREET
STEWART STREET
HOWARD STREET
A STREET

7

district for a time. Thereafter, prostitutes resumed their usual behavior, luring men by exposing themselves, calling, whistling, etc.

Prostitutes were often arrested for drunken and disorderly conduct and vulgar language. They usually received minor fines and allowed to go. Some prostitutes stole from customers and were arrested when caught. Black Hills Kate was a notorious thief. Arrested several times for theft, Kate was asked to leave town. She refused and was jailed for 100 days.

Some prostitutes stole mining stocks from customers. Madam Rachel stole thirty shares of Mexican Mine stock from a mill workman.

Prostitution was a large and accepted part of life in Virginia City for several reasons. First, there were few women, single or married.

Second, there was little for miners to do in their off hours except gamble, drink and visit houses of prostitution. Most miners squandered their money and were unable to save up enough to bring wives and girl friends to Virginia City.

Third, many men visited houses of prostitution not only for sex but for female attention and entertainment. Not every visit to a house of prostitution led to intercourse. Many men enjoyed the gay, party atmosphere of the whorehouse. There was music, singing and the girls did their best to make each man feel welcome. Men received attention at a whorehouse. Madams noted that this was often more important to men than sex. Female attention gave miners relief from their loneliness and tension.

Fourth, the danger of working and living in Virginia City drove men to prostitutes. Deep mining was extremely dangerous. Everyday there were injuries and horrible deaths in the mines. Alfred Doten, a Virginia City journalist who kept a detailed journal of life in Virgnina City wrote of one mining accident, "...9 more bodies recovered today — some 3 or 4 I saw... had heads crushed horribly — one had his head torn entirely off — 20 corpses so far..." Doten wrote of another accident, "...At 11 Dr. Hiller came with his buggy, & took me down to Hospital... Wm. Neely a deaf & dumb miner there, who had his right shoulder broken by a cave in... He was knocked down through 2 floors — some 15 ft. — badly bruised & skinned up besides — We opened his shoulder & found the bone all smashed up — Removed all the upper part of arm bone from shoulder socket down — some dozen or more pieces of it — down half way to elbow — full 8 inches of the bone gone — flesh badly lacerated — man will probably die..."

Miners saw this sort of accident daily. In addition, life in Virginia City saloons, gambling places and whorehouses was dangerous. Hard drinking led to much violence. Doten wrote, "... About 5 PM Myles Goodman shot & killed Al P. Waterman at the Delta Saloon... 4 bullet holes, left groin, right breast near nipple, left side of windpipe and top of head — died at once." For a long time the town was tough; gun and knife fights were common.

Danger and fear of death drove men to prostitutes. Nell Kimball, the 19th century New Orleans madam, noted that in times of war, the whorehouse business boomed. She claimed men — especially soldiers — saught relief from fear of death in sex.

Virginia City, Nevada, taken during the boom period of the 1870's, looking west toward Mt. Davidson. The California Pan Mill is in the foreground. Gold and silver were discovered in Gold Canyon in 1859. Virginia City first boomed in the early 1860's petered out but was revived in the early 1870's when the Big Bonanza was struck. Nevada Historical Society

"Sporting Row," or the primary Virginia City redlight district on D Street. Shown here in this 1924 photo are cribs along the west side of D Street looking south. The large four story brick building is the Frederick House at the corner of Union and D Streets. Julia Bulette's cottage stood across the street at the northeast corner of Union and D Streets. Special Collections, University of Nevada, Reno

Shown here are the local Virginia City and Gold Hill newspaper reporters. Dan DeQuille, in the middle, was a friend of Mark Twain and highly influenced the young writer. Alfred Doten, seated at far right, kept a daily journal which gives insight into the daily goings on in Virginia City. Special Collections, University of Nevada, Reno

Virginia City from the north end. The arrow points to the north D Street area where Cad Thompson's "Brick" parlour house was located across from the V and T freight depot. Nevada Historical Society

The Prostitutes

The women who worked in the redlight districts came from all parts of the world. An 1875 census showed that ⅔ were foreign born. In 1880, 54% were foreign born. Many prostitutes' names reflected their nationality: Irish Blonde, Spanish Liz, Dutch Mary, English Gussie and Jew Annie were typical.

French women were considered the most attractive because they lived fast. American women were the next most attractive.

There were many Spanish and Mexican prostitutes. Famines in Central America and South America drove these women into prostitution. Some indentured themselves to ship captains for passage to the United States. Afterwards, they worked in shanty towns and in the California mining camps. Spanish and Mexican prostitutes were considered less attractive because of the color of their skin. Most worked by themselves in cribs or in small, lower class brothels.

There were a few black prostitutes. They and the Chinese women were considered the least attractive and worked in the worst places.

According to the 1880 census, half of all redlight women had been married. Thirty-one were married, 27 were widowed and 12 were divorced. The married women no longer lived with their husbands.

Most of those prostitutes who had been married were deserted by their husbands or were beaten by them. Some had had husbands who were unfaithful and they had left them. Three wives left husbands and immediately went to work in the red light district. One woman took the household furniture while her husband was away. When the husband returned, he retrieved his furniture but left his wife where she was.

Prostitutes ranged in ages from 13 to 60. Sixty-eight percent were under 30, mostly 19-29. Thirty-one percent were 30-60. A small group were 18 or under, the majority, Chinese women. Authorities and moral societies generally did not permit white girls under 18 to work in houses of prostitution. Efforts were made to return underage girls to their parents or find suitable homes.

There were two stories of underage girls that made the papers. Maghey Gorhey, 13, was drugged by her mother and forced to work in Nellie Sayers saloon-brothel on the Barbary Coast. Another girl, a 15 year old, went to work for the infamous Rose Benjamin because here home life was worse than life in a whorehouse. These stories, however, were unusual.

Why So Many Prostitutes?

In 1875, 307 women worked in Virginia City's redlight district. One out of every 12 women was a prostitute. As the mines slowed down in 1880, 146 women worked in the districts.

Poverty and lack of jobs for women were the major reasons women became prostitutes in Virginia City, throughout America and Europe during the 19th century.

During the 19th century the man was the center of the family and of society. A married man's duty was to provide food, shelter, clothing, money and emotional stability for his family. It was the man who went out into the world to earn his living.

His wife stayed at home, bore children, cared for them, cooked and cleaned her home. In her home, she was protected by her husband from the harshness of the outside world.

But when a woman did not or could not marry or when she was widowed or divorced and had no relatives with whom she could live, she found herself in an extremely precarious position. She was then forced to work. The jobs available to working women were low and poorly paid, mostly sweatshop labor and domestic service as cooks, maids, house cleaner, seamstress and a few school teaching positions. A woman was required to work for long hours and low pay.

In addition, women who had to work were not respected by other women and men. As Nell Kimball, the 19th century New Orleans madam wrote, "Wages were low for women... and no one had much respect for a girl who had to work. Believe me it's the Good People who exploit poor girls who make a lot of whores."

If a woman had children her position was even more difficult. She had the burdern of working long hours, finding childcare, then coming home to the children, having to cook, feed and bathe them. It was an awesome burden.

Prostitution became an attractive alternative for uncared for poor women. Except for street walkers, prostitutes with children could work out of their homes, they were safer in their homes than on the street, the pay was fair to terrific and they were able to care for their children. Thousands of poor women chose prostitution as a means of surviving. As Nell Kimball wrote, "Most of the girls who went into parlour houses had found themselves in the city, hungry, no job, no rent money, clothes getting tattered... There was never much problem in getting them to see the advantage of a good house and a square meal. All the rest is bleeding sentimentality by people who don't know whores."

Once seduced into a life of prostitution, many prostitutes from the east coast and from all parts of the world were lured to the mining camps and railroad towns of the American West for the hope of good pay.

Types of Houses of Prostitution

There were four types of houses of prostitution in Virginia City: 1) the parlour house with the prettiest girls, handsomest surroundings, best liquor and music, and of course, the highest price; 2) the brothel, a lower quality house usually operated by a madam with two or more girls; 3) cribs, where a girl worked alone in a small one or two room shack and 4) Barbary Coast dives, where women drank with customers and had sex with them in the back bedrooms.

In addition, there were many street walkers who flaunted themselves on C Street, usually near the corners of C and Union Street. Having lured a customer, street walkers usually took them back to their rooms, sometimes

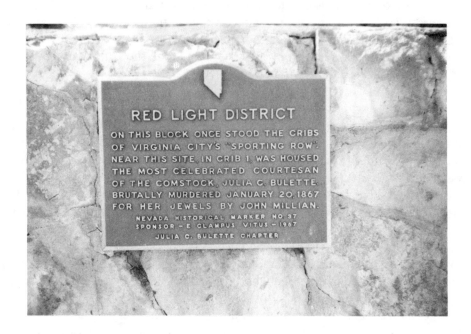

Above, an historical marker placed by E. Clampus Vitus on D Street. Below, the last remaining crib on D Street.

located in a lodging house, hotel, crib, brothel or parlour house.

There were also many girls who worked in melodeons and saloons as waitresses, dancers, entertainers, who offered themselves for money. These women usually met their customers at work and took them home afterwards.

The Prostitution Hierarchy

At the top of the prostitution ladder were the profiteers and landlords. These were men who owned land or houses which madams and prostitutes leased or rented. Sometimes these men were silent partners with madams as was J.A. Batchelor who earned 5% of Jessie Lester's parlour house. Most of these landlords were wealthy and had other careers.

John Piper was typical. He owned Piper's Opera House, for many years Virginia City's chief entertainment establishment. He had been Virginia City's mayor and later Nevada State Senator. Yet, he was publicly lambasted by a journalist for owning brothel land and thwarting efforts to create legislation that would set boundaries for redlight districts. Virginia City's D Street redlight was often referred to as Piper's Row.

Next came the saloon owners and managers who sometimes allowed prostitutes in their establishments or directed customers up the stairs or into backrooms. There were, of course, many high toned saloons that did not allow prostitutes on the premises nor were they affiliated with prostitution activity.

Next were the madams. These were usually middle-aged and older women, many of whom were once prostitutes. Madams were shrewd businesswomen, good managers and highly respected by businessmen. A madam either rented or purchased a house. She hired the girls, bought furniture, beds and bedding, hired a cook, bouncer, bartender, musicians and disciplined her girls when they got out of hand. It was a demanding and complicated job. She was hostess to her customers and was responsible for graciously obtaining their money. A madam also had to shrewdly politic police and authorities.

Madams received a percentage of each girl's earnings, usually 25-50%. Some madams rented out rooms to girls. These girls were called "boarders" and madams were often referred to as "landladies." A boarding prostitute was free to walk the street if necessary and take customers back to her room. Or, she could rely on the madam to provide her customers.

Madams generally did not compete with their girls for customers. They were less promiscuous. Most took lovers, some were even married. Because they were shrewd and less promiscuous, they were respected by the prostitution demimonde and by respectable men as well.

Some of Virginia City's most well known madams were Cad Thompson, Rose Benjamin, Jessie Lester, Jenny Tyler, Molly Ashton, Madam Rey, Liz Hays and Nellie Sayers.

Next were women who ran saloon-brothels, most of which were on the Barbary Coast. Mit Raymond, 56, ran a one woman saloon-brothel on the Barbary Coast. When she died she left a large estate which included her Virginia

City saloon, a saloon in San Francisco and land in Oakland, Sacramento and Marysville worth $40,000, a very large sum in those days.

Last of the profiteers were the pimps. A pimp was a man who earned all or part of his living from a prostitute. Pimps often competed or worked in collusion with madams. A pimp was also called a "masher", "ponce", "sport", "gentlemen of leisure" or a prostitute's "man" or "lover." Pimps provided prostitutes with an illusion of romance and affection in exchange for money. Pimps accompanied their prostitutes to restaurants, saloons, whore balls, music halls and opium dens. A pimp usually demanded that his girl earn a certain quota each night. If a girl did well, she was given affection. If not, she was denied affection, beaten or scolded. Many pimps used liquor or drugs — laudanum and cocaine the most popular — to manipulate and enslave their women.

In 1875, there were 38 men who lived in brothels or with individual women. In 1880, there were 9. Most pimps were between 35 and 40 years of age.

Two pages of a letter written by a Mrs. Carr to Rosa May in Virginia City. Mrs. Carr inquires about her daughter's strange death. Her daughter, Marie Nenninger, was a prostitute. Mrs. Carr thanked Rosa May and the other girls for seeing that her daughter received a proper burial.

Rosa May, parlour house prostitute and call girl. For many years Rosa May worked at Cad Thompson's "Brick" parlour house at 56 North D Street. Like other prostitutes she shuttled back and forth between Carson and Virginia City. During the months she lived in Carson, Ernest Marks, her lover wrote frequently. The author discovered their love letters. Photo taken about 1879 when Rosa May was 24.

Order Of Prostitutes

Even in the demimonde (underworld) of prostitution, there were class distinctions. Prostitutes could be cast into four groups: 1) elite, 2) middle rank, 3) working and 4) lower class.

The elite were not full time prostitutes. They were women — usually very successful actresses or entertainers — who used sex to keep a man, say as a mistress or women who conned men into giving them money without giving sex. Elite prostitutes were highly selective of their customers, usually wealthy businessmen. They were discrete, expensive and coy as to how they obtained payment for their services.

Middle rank prostitutes were attractive and did not actively solicit customers. They were discrete and relied on word of mouth for business. They worked indoors where men came to them. They did not walk the streets. Middle rank prostitutes were able to choose the men with whom they had sex. They were able to reject violent or men ridden with venereal disease. Some worked as waiter girls and entertainers in melodeons — the Alhambra Theater and the Villa de Belvelier the most well known. Some worked in gambling houses, large saloons and dance halls. Melodeon girls entertained on stage in bawdy plays, waiter girls served drinks and sometimes drank with customers, dance hall girls danced with customers for a small fee. Most establishments permitted girls to run their own business. But some, like the Alhambra Theater and the Villa de Belvelier, had small private rooms where singers and actresses had sex with customers. Other middle rank prostitutes worked in parlour houses, better brothels or worked alone in cottages.

Middle rank prostitutes sold companionship and fun as well as sex. They usually saw one customer a night. Middle rank prostitutes were able to support themselves well but most never made enough to leave prostitution altogether. The legendary Julia Bulette, who was murdered, was a middle rank prostitute. Her story will be told shortly.

Middle rank girls who worked in parlour houses were the most fortunate. In 1880, there were four parlour houses on D street. Two had 5 girls and two had 4 girls. Parlour house girls were young, usually between 18 and 32, attractive and well paid. They usually made $10-20 per customer although the madam took 25-50%. This still left the girl with $5-$15. Keep in mind that miners risked their lives in grueling 8-10 hour shifts for $4 a day, $20 a week, and this was considered good pay. The percentage the madam took covered a girl's rent, food, cooking, laundry, liquor and protection.

Most of the girls who worked in parlour houses were from North America, Great Britain and France. As long as they were young, attractive and controlled themselves on the job, they were able to travel a circuit of parlour houses which included Carson City, Virginia City, Reno and neighboring mining towns.

Rosa May was a typical parlour house girl. She worked for many years in Cad Thompson's "Brick house" a gaudy, three story house at 56 North D Street.

Rosa May was young, attractive and intelligent. Whenever Cad Thompson was away, she put Rosa May in charge of her house.

Rosa May moved to the mining camp of Bodie, California in 1892 after Thompson closed the Brick house after thirty-two years of operation. In Bodie the well respected and kind hearted Rosa May died while nursing miners during an epidemic. Several years ago the author discovered Rosa May's outcast grave in Bodie which led him to a 3½ year search for Rosa May's story. This culminated in the book, ROSA MAY: THE SEARCH FOR A MINING CAMP LEGEND. The author located letters written to Rosa May in Virginia City between 1876-80, one of which was written by Cad Thompson herself. This and twenty-five other letters and historic photos are included in ROSA MAY. A movie of Rosa May's life is now planned.

In ROSA MAY, the author describes a day in the parlour girl's life:

The occupational hazards and torment of the prostitute's life were insufferable. Consider one of her days:

She wakes in the early afternoon and comes downstairs for coffee. She never feels like eating much and the madam has to force her to eat breakfast.

She sits or lies about during the afternoon, plays cards, gossips with the other girls. Usually she has no interests and may begin to drink. Sometimes, she goes shopping, buys a new dress, hat, jewelry or perfume.

In the early evening, she dresses in a fine gown, but nothing too fancy. When the johns arrive, the madam calls her and five or six other girls downstairs. The johns may be repeat customers or strangers.

The girl goes into her act: she is sweet, she is pretty, she is dumb, she is willing, she has no needs, she is a servant, she'll do whatever any man wants.

She sits with the other girls beside their customers at the long mahogany dining table. The talk is gay, the other girls giggle, she giggles too. The men are buying and pouring champagne, $20 a bottle. The madam is charming, witty, strong, in control.

Dinner finished, the girls and johns move into the parlour. There is a bar where a brawny bouncer serves as bartender. The girls and johns sip drinks.

She is gay and cool as she makes her hustle. Finally, one of the men chooses her. She leads him up the stairs by the hand, one hand on the banister, to her room and the big bed. She does anything he wants her to do and says anything he wants her to say. If the john is a repeat customer, she knows his needs and goes about her business self-assured. This is one thing in life she knows she does well. She moans, but is not aroused. It is all an act, but it is thoroughly convincing. As she goes through the motions, she hopes he will come soon so she can get on to the next customer. But she does not rush him, bad business, it would hurt his feelings and ruin his tip.

The arrow points to Cad Thompson's three story "Brick" parlour house at 56 North D Street. Thompson operated this house from the early 1860's until 1892 when she sold out. Adjacent buildings are houses of prostitution. Special Collections. University of Nevada, Reno

It's over. She washes the john down with hot water and soap. If he picks up anything, he'll know he didn't get it from her. She smiles and jokes as she washes. The john is drunk and feels relieved after the workout. She helps him dress. As he leaves he palms a gold coin on her dresser. She smiles and thanks him.

Immediately the girl begins to douche. There are several to choose from: lysol, bichloride of mercury, mercuric cyanide, carbolic acid and potassium permanganate. Afterwards, the girl dresses and combs her hair. The maid rushes in to change the sheets and make the bed for the next john.

Meanwhile, the john has gone downstairs and the madam has graciously collected the $20, part of which belongs to the girl. The madam asks if he is pleased. He is.

The john either leaves but more often stays to visit with the other johns, many of whom he knows or does business with. The parlour house is sort of a social club, they meet here often, sometimes just to visit the girls and other men. Sometimes the men play poker, but the girls try to steer them away from gambling. They know men prefer gambling to screwing.

The girl comes downstairs and begins to hustle another customer... rarely will one arouse her.

She may work as late as five or six in the morning. Sometimes a john will stay the night. If none stay the night and work is over, she goes out with her pimp or with other girls to a restaurant. Over food and coffee, the girls discuss their various customers, especially the weird ones.

If the girl has a pimp, she'll hand over most of her night's earnings. If she has done well, the pimp will be pleased and will treat her kindly. If she hasn't done well, he may beat, scold, or deny her affection. She tries to do well so her pimp will be pleased and be nice to her. Her pimp is everything to her, her God, her master, her lover. As abnormal as it seems, her relationship with him is the most important human contact she has.

If the girl does not have a pimp, she's probably blue. All night men have pawed and used her and not one has given a damn about her feelings. She may start to drink hard, snuff "snow" (cocaine) or take laudanum, a liquid preparation of opium, to ease the pain of her loneliness. If she goes low enough, she may kill herself, which is not uncommon. If not, she'll return to the house, sleep until the next afternoon, waking to repeat the same routine that hardly ever changes. One day a week she is given off to spend with her pimp or go where she likes. She is like a little girl living at home under strict rules. Responsibility for her life is put in someone else's hands, at least temporarily.

Such was the whore's routine, years without thought, planning or meaning. It was a rare girl, who, after some years in the trade, lived a normal happy life. Many were constantly depressed, eventually cracked up or killed themselves. Suicide was a haunting demon in every whorehouse.

The loneliness of a prostitute's life, even the high class parlour house girl, was immense. Cut off from her family by disgrace, the resulting shame and loneliness was awesome. She had placed herself in a world where she was used by everyone: by customers, madams, pimps, and often lesbian lovers.

To add to her troubles, there was the constant threat of pregnancy or disease, Little Casino (gonorrhea) or Big Casino (syphilis.) And there were always the crazies; overly polite men who cracked their knuckles and beat or killed prostitutes whenever they had the chance.

The life was hard on a girl and wore her down physically, emotionally and spiritually. Unlike other professions, a prostitute's money making years were few. She started at top pay and her earnings decreased as her youth and beauty faded.

A girl, at best, lasted half a dozen years in a quality parlour house. After that, she usually became a street hooker, whispering arousing offers, exposing herself on street corners. The parlour house girl, who had been protected by the madam, well fed and clothed, and known the best customers, found street hustling terribly humiliating. As Dolly Fine, another madam, once said, "There is nothing more pitiful in life than a prostitute who has risen from the streets, tasted luxuries and like them, and then finds herself once again in the gutter." Rather than live with the fall, many fading prostitutes chose suicide.

Mrs. Leconey's boarding house was located here in this building at 31 N. C. Street. Here Isaac Isaacs, a merchant lived. Isaacs was a customer of Rosa May's. Isaacs wrote notes to Rosa May and requested that she come to his room.

The largest group of Virginia City prostitutes, at least 50%, were "working" prostitutes. These women worked out of cribs, saloons, hotels, lodging houses and smaller brothels. In 1880, there were two brothels with 3 women each, nine houses had 2 women and 12 women worked alone in cribs. Compared to middle rank prostitutes, working girls made a bare living. They lacked the looks, personality and charm of the middle rank girls. Working prostitutes sold impersonal sex; most charged one dollar for a short visit. Working girls tried to turn as many "tricks" per night as possible. When men did not come to them, working girls searched the streets for customers. Most hung around the corners of C Street and Union. Here they paraded themselves between 4 and 8 p.m. Some exposed themselves, whispered offers, whistled or shouted obscenities. Working girls were looked down on by the respectable as well as by other prostitutes because they actively solicited prostitution, were indiscrete, sold impersonal sex and earned less. Working girls made enough to live on but rarely owned property or willed property when they died. Their lives were more public than middle rank prostitutes and newspapers frequently carried items about their crimes, brawls and suicides.

Clara Howard, a prostitute at D and Sutton, shot herself after a quarrel with her lover.

Nellie Ross, living at Carson and B Street, aged 28, committed suicide by taking laudanum. Jealousy over her lover the reason.

Frankie Norton took twelve grains of laudanum. She was saved by Dr. Carter who pumped her stomach. Said she has nothing to live for. Has tried to kill herself in the past, swears to try again.

Ida Vernon, 32, killed herself with an overdose of chloroform. A man who had spent the night with her found her dead beside him in bed in the morning.

The last group were lower class or "prostitutes of the lowest order" as journalists frequently labeled them. A large portion of these were Chinese, Mexican, Spanish and black women. Some of the lower class prostitutes were white vagrants — drunks or drug addicts who sold sex for very little or for drugs or alcohol.

Rose Wilson was a typical white, vagrant prostitute. She was notorious and the Enterprise frequently carried items about her latest exploits. At one time she had been the wife of a miner and had several children. After Rose's husband was killed in the mines, she turned to drink. When sober, Rose was kind, drunk she became a hell raiser breaking windows, shouting obscenities and brawling. She was often found passed out in the gutter. Policemen often arrested her just to give her a warm place to sleep.

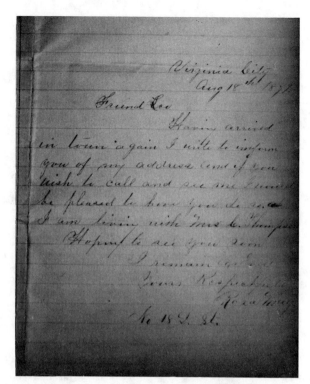

bove, a letter written by Rosa May to Leo Miller, a jeweler. The handwriting was analyzed by pro-
ssional graphoanalysts and much was learned about Rosa May's personality. Below, an envelope
ddressed to Rosa May in Carson City.

This is a pencil written letter by Emma, perhaps Emma Goldsmith. Emma says that it must be nice for Rosa May to go out at night and make a "shining $20." Emma mentions other prostitutes and madams as well as Mr. Brooks, a Carson merchant and customer.

A love letter written by Ernest Marks June 12, 1879 to Rosa May then working in Carson City. Notice Marks' deep, dark writing. This reveals that Marks was a passionate man capable of great affection and violence.

The Madams

Cad Thompson ran a three story parlour house at 56 North D Street between Sutton and Mill Street called the "Brick house". Thompson ran several houses of prostitution in Virginia City from the early 1860's until 1892.

Cad Thompson was born in Ireland in 1827. She was a widow who had a son, Henry, who later killed himself. Cad was a typical parlour house madam. She was tough, practical, had a good sense of humor and at times got out of control. Numerous times she was arrested for drunken and disorderly conduct. She was stubborn too. On several occasions she refused to pay her fines and chose jail instead.

June 6, 1885, the Virginia City Chronicle carried these humorous lines:

While sitting at the second-story window of her establishment on D street, last Saturday evening, the widow Thompson observed a young man whom she recognized as the 'Barbary Coast masher,' [pimp] holding a rope behind him and trying to coax her dog away, which was sitting in the doorway. Arming herself with a large bucketful of slops, she waited until the masher grasped the dog by the collar, when she emptied the entire contents of the bucket on his person. Adonis let go his hold and lit out in the direction of the north pole, closely followed by the affronted dog and at least half a dozen fleet footed female denizens of the Thompson 'mayzong,' armed with mops and stove pokers.

November 18, 1866, Alf. Doten wrote in his journal that Cad Thompson had been the victim of a cruel joke:

Some fellows took No. 1's engine about 4 o'clock this morning and washed out old Cad Thompson's whore house — gave her hell — created quite a consternation among the law and order portion of the community — not the end of it yet — We shall have to see who rules the city now the rough or the decent men.

The Territorial Enterprise of February 17, 1875, revealed that Cad's real name was Sarah Hagan. Hagan was taken to court by Andrew Allison in an effort to repossess his house in the redlight. What the circumstances were are not clear. Hagan fought Allison bitterly for a month but lost the case.

Cad Thompson's Brick house was the finest and most popular parlour house in Virginia City. Journalists Alf Doten and Dan DeQuille frequented her place, often just for entertainment and conversation.

Thompson had a lover, Harry , and a house handyman, George. When she was away, she put Rosa May in charge. In a letter from Thompson to Rosa May written in San Francisco March 27, 1880, Thompson, then 53, complained of her rheumatism. She may have gone to San Francisco to escape Virginia City's cold winter. She also complained that it would be difficult to find new girls to work her house in Virginia City. By 1880, Virginia City's mines were

Above, Mary Ann Phillips' house in Virginia City. Though Phillips ran a Carson City brothel where Rosa May at times worked, Phillips lived in Virginia City here with her family. Below, the grave of Mary Ann Phillips in Carson's Lone Mountain Cemetery.

petering out and the long decline had begun. Brothel owners felt the pinch as miners were laid off and left town for new camps. Depressed, Thompson did not want to return to her "damp, dreary house" but admitted she would have to go back.

Thompson finally sold out in Virginia City in 1892 at the age of 65. She had lived and worked in Virginia City for more than thirty years. It is believed she moved to San Francisco where she died. The author attempted to locate Thompson's death record and burial site but many public records were destroyed in San Francisco's Great Fire of 1906.

Jessie Lester was another popular madam. She purchased her two story house on D Street from J.A. Batchellor for $2000 plus 5% of the house earnings. Jessie's house was 32 feet wide and of unknown depth. There were two parlours downstairs and five bedrooms upstairs. The house was without a kitchen, dining room or indoor plumbing. Both parlours had chandeliers and windows were decorated wth lace curtains. Brussels carpets covered the cold wooden floors and antimacassars were draped over the backs and arms of chairs to protect them. Each parlour had a sofa and about five chairs each.

Jessie's upstairs bedroom consisted of a matched mahogany bedroom set, a marble topped washstand, bureau, bedstead and lamp tables. Her bed had a spring mattress and on top of this a horsehair mattress. There was a spitoon and basin for waste.

Jessie Lester was shot by an unknown man December 19, 1864. Though she lived another month, she never told police who shot her. Alf Doten was with Jessie when her arm was amputated. He wrote in his diary December 27:

had to have her right arm amputated at the shoulder joint this afternoon — poor creature, she was just recovering from the taking of chloroform during the operation and was shrieking with pain — and in her delirium, calling on her mother...

Jessie was aware she was going to die. During her last month she paid her remaining bills, gave her personal things away, made her will and planned her funeral. She died 6 a.m. January 23, 1865.

Prostitutes and madams were always buried outside the regular cemeteries. But Jessie Lester managed to be buried in Virginia City's Catholic cemetery. This likely came about because Jessie left the bulk of her estate, $5294, to the Sisters of Charity. This probably bought Jessie the privilege of a Catholic burial. Jessie's ill-gained money went to care for orphans.

The popular Father Manogue gave Jessie her last rights and held funeral services at St. Mary's of the Mountains. Jessie's funeral procession consisted of a half dozen carriages "filled with whores," Doten wrote.

The author searched for Jessie's grave in the Catholic portion of the cemetery but could not find it. Jessie's grave marker was likely stolen; many graves have been vandalized.

Rose Benjamin for twelve years ran an average brothel at 15-15½ North D

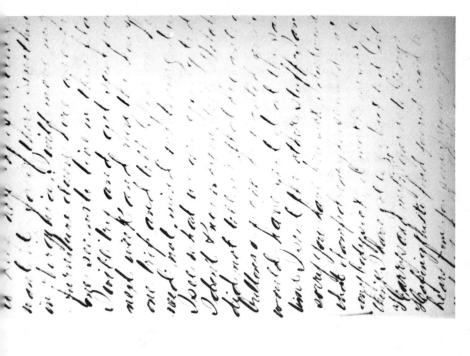

A letter written by Cad Thompson March 27, 1880 in San Francisco and addressed to Rosa May, then in charge of Thompson's "Brick." Thompson complains of the slow times in Virginia City and how difficult it will be to get new girls to work there. She regrets that she must return to her "damp, dreary house."

Street on the west side of D between Union and Sutton Avenue, a few doors north of Mollinelli's hotel. She owned four houses of prostitution in a row. Unlike some madams, Rose lived outside the redlight district in a respectable neighborhood. Though everyone knew how she earned her living, she still kept her brothel land under her niece's name. Phil Escobar worked for Rose and ran her business when she was away.

Rose was hard on her girls. Three girls committed suicide while working for Rose and several others made attempts. One suicide, Scotch Laura, real name Laura Steel, killed herself early one morning after Rose's all night birthday party. Laura was a beautiful 22 year old with black hair and fair skin. She was born in Scotland and came to America with her brother and sister. Laura later moved to Virginia City with her husband, a saloon keeper. Six months before her death, she left her husband. She changed her name and went to work at Rose's.

Rose searched for and hired young girls to work in her brothel. She took in Miss Duffy, a 15 year old. Rose also persuaded 16 year old, Hattie Willis, of the Amelia Dean Melodeon Troup to leave the company and come to work for her. As many as seven girls worked for Rose at one time.

Rose Benjamin had an uncanny way of getting publicity. Newspapers frequently carried her exploits. Some items were dramatic. Several fires at her houses drew great attention. One fire was started by a vindictive former lover. Others were believed set by Rose herself so she could collect insurance money.

In 1878, at the age of 36, Rose married her lover, George E. Perkins. Shortly after, Rose left Virginia City for unknown parts.

Nellie (Ellen) Sayers ran a lower class saloon-brothel on the Barbary Coast at 146½ South C Street. An Enterprise journalist called Nellie, "the worst specimen of femininity ever to crawl down C Street." She lied, cheated, robbed; she was a drunk and a whore. Her saloon was a low, one story building which she rented. The front part was a barroom with a kitchen and two bedrooms in the rear. Three girls worked for Nellie, some were very young. Maghey Gorhey was 13, Susie Brown, 15.

Next to Nellie Sayer's was Peter Larkin's at 146 South C Street. Daniel Corcoran and his wife ran another saloon-brothel at 158 South C Street. Peter Larkin, Daniel Corcoran and Nellie became involved in a love triangle that ended in Corcoran's murder and Larkin being hanged.

In June, 1877, Peter Larkin, Nellie's estranged lover and neighbor, caught Nellie and Daniel Corcoran in bed. Larkin shot and killed Corcoran though some believed Nellie killed Corcoran herself.

Nellie and a witness, Susie Brown, charged Larkin with Corcoran's murder and testified against him in court. Nellie was drunk most of the trial and frequently changed her story. Still, the jury found Larkin guilty and sentenced him to be hanged. Larkin appealed to the Nevada Supreme Court but the court upheld Larkin's verdict.

Larkin was hanged as sentenced. Due to much public feeling against her,

Nellie Sayers was forced to leave town. This closed another Barbary Coast dive during the 1877 cleanup campaign.

There were other madams but newspapers gave little information about them. Molly Ashton, Inez, Mary Blane, Liz Hayes, China Mary and a man called Weston ran houses of prostitution. Jenny Tyler ran the popular "Bow Windows" parlour house which Alf Doten and Dan DeQuille frequented. Madam Reyes had a brothel at 15 North D Street at one time where she employed six Mexican women.

Peter Larkin, who ran a saloon-brothel on the Barbary Coast. Larkin, Nellie Sayers' estranged lover, murdered Daniel Corcoran, a rival for Nellie's affections. Larkin was found guilty of murder and hanged. Special Collections, University of Nevada, Reno

Above, a rare photo of Chinese prostitutes and a child. Below, the Frederick House. The Alhambra Theater, a bawdy melodeon, was located on the first floor. Cribs are in background. Special Collections, University of Nevada, Reno and Nevada Historical Society.

The Murder of Julia Bulette

January 20, 1867, the bloody body of Julia Bulette was found in her bed. She had been beaten and strangled. It was, "The most cruel, outrageous and revolting murder ever committed in this city...," wrote a journalist. The entire Virginia City detective force was assigned to the case and the search for Julia's murderer began.

Julia Bulette was a 35 year old middle rank prostitute. She lived alone in a small, two room white cottage in the heart of the redlight district at No. 4 North D Street near the northeast corner of Union and D. She had lived in Virginia City for five years. Though she had a French name, Julia was born in England, some accounts say London, others Liverpool. She came to America as a young woman with her brother and settled in New Orleans where she married a man named Smith from whom she was separated. It is not known why or how she became a prostitute.

Julia came to California in 1852-53 during the gold rush. She lived in various California mining towns until 1863 when she arrived in Virginia City.

For a prostitute, Julia Bulette was unusually well liked by the demimonde as well as by respectable men. Julia was extraordinarily kind and gave much of her time and money to helping others. She contributed considerable money to Virginia Engine Co. No. 1 and the fireman made her an honorary member. There were times she accompanied the firemen to fires and even worked the brakes of the engine. "...Few of her class had more true friends," a journalist wrote.

As a popular middle rank prostitute, Julia Bulette earned a good living. She dressed well, drank the best liquor and paid her bills. She was never a madam as some writers have claimed nor did she live in a large luxurious mansion. She sold comanionship and sex and usually spent the entire night with one customer. Many well known men considered her a friend and often visited her for friendship and conversation. Alf Doten wrote in his journal of his visits with Julia.

Julia's two room cottage had a front room and a rear bedroom. The front room could hold a dozen people. Her bedroom had a large mahogany bed, two wash basins and a spitoon. The cottage was without a kitchen and indoor plumbing.

For three months prior to her death, Julia Bulette had been ill. She had stayed a month in Carson City with her friend, Annie Smith, a prostitute. Annie had given Julia a piece of gold jewelery which she wanted repaired in Virginia City. This item would later be found in the possession of John Millian, Julia's accused murderer.

A week before her death, Julia's health improved and she returned to Virginia City. It snowed that week, then the snow turned into rain and the streets were clogged with mud.

Saturday evening, January 19, Julia went to Piper's Opera House on B

The legendary Julia Bulette, murdered Januray 20, 1867. Julia stands beside a helmet belonging to Virginia Engine Company No. 1 of which Julia had been made an honorary member. Julia Bulette was clearly a white English woman. Right, a Creole woman whom some writers and historians claim was Julia Bulette. Newspaper reports of the day prove that Julia was not a Creole. Nevada Historical Society.

Street to see a comedy, Willful Murder, and a play, The Robbers. She was not allowed entrance at the front door because she was a prostitute. Rather than sit in the section of the theater set aside for the redlight women, Julia went home.

The last person to see Julia alive was Gertrude Holmes, a friend and prostitute who lived one door away at No. 6 North D Street. At 11:30 p.m. Julia stopped at Gertrude's and said she was expecting a man at midnight who had made plans to spend the night. Julia did not mention the man's name. A newspaper boy passing by Julia's at 5 a.m. the following morning reported that he heard a woman scream once.

At 11:30 the next morning, Gertrude went to Julia's to invite her for breakfast. Gertrude found Julia's front door locked and went to the rear where she found the back door open. Gertrude called for Julia and when there was no answer she entered the house. She found Julia dead in her bed. There was a pillow squashed against Julia's face. When Gertrude removed the pillow, she found the bed underneath Julia's head saturated with blood. Julia was naked. Her dress lay on the floor next to her bed where she had stepped out of it. One side of the bed was smooth as if she had spent the night alone.

Gertrude ran from the house screaming. A crowd soon gathered by Julia's cottage.

J.R. Kaneen was the first man on the murder scene. He testified at the coroner's jury that he found Julia's body cold and stiff. Her contorted form, bruises and finger nail lacerations on her throat, and a wound on Julias head, led Kaneen to believe that Julia was first beaten with a stick of wood and then strangled. Kaneen found pieces of cedar wood in Julia's hair, on the bedspread and a bloody stick of wood lay beside her bed. Doctors Bronson and Gaston performed an autopsy. Removing the scalp, they discoverd the skull had not been injured. The brain was congested; the doctors concluded Julia Bulette died from strangulation.

Julia Bulette's funeral followed on Monday, January 21. At 3 p.m. 60 men from Virginia Engine Company No. 1, proceeded south down C Street led by the Metropolitan Brass Band toward the Flowery Hill Cemetery, a cemetery reserved for outcasts east of town. The hearse was followed by 18 carriages filled with Julia's friends, mostly prostitutes. The sky was somber and grey and it began to snow and rain. At the edge of town, the men from Engine Company No. 1 stepped aside and the procession went ahead without them to the Flowery Hill Cemetery about a mile and a half away.

The murderer of Julia Bulette left no clues to his identity. Though the entire Virginia City detective force searched several months for the murderer, they concluded the murderer had likely left Virginia City and escaped.

But several months later, Martha Camp, a prostitute, was awakened by a burglar with a knife. Martha screamed, the intruder fled but she had gotten

Hank Monk, the famous stage driver. He was a personal friend of Julia Bulette's.

38

a good look at his face. Shortly afterwards, Martha Camp saw the burglar on C Street. He was arrested and charged with attempted robbery and murder.

The man was John Millian, a Frenchman who spoke very little English. He was about 35, large and heavily built. He spoke with a coarse sonorous voice. Other Frenchmen reportedly disliked Millian because he was a braggart. He was reported to have known Julia Bulette, having done laundry for the slain prostitute.

While John Millian was in jail, a Mrs. Fisher came forward. She had purchased a dress pattern from a man for $40 though the pattern was worth $60. She identified John Millian as the man who sold her the pattern. Sam Rosener, a dry goods merchant who had sold the unique pattern to Julia Bulette, identified the pattern as the one he had sold to Julia.

May 25, 1867, the newspapers reported that John Millian had been charged with the murder of Julia Bulette. Chief of Police Edwards had found Julia's trunk behind a D Street bakery owned by M. Ardent. The bakery was located across from Julia Bulette's house. The trunk had been left there by Millian and contained Julia's clothing and jewelery.

When Chief Edwards showed Millian the items found in the trunk, Millian reportedly confessed to the murder. He said he didn't want to live and asked Edwards to blow his brains out. Afterwards, Millian said he wanted to be hanged as soon as possible. Later, he denied this confession.

John Millian, the 35 year old Frenchman who murdered Julia Bulette. Newspapers claimed Millian had done laundry for Bulette. Special Collections, University of Nevada, Reno.

Millian later said that two men and he went to Bulette's to rob her. One of the men was Chris Blair. Chris Blair was found in San Francisco and arrested. Sheriff George Downey brought Blair back to Virginia City. But when Chris Blair was brought into the same room as Millian, Millian failed to identify him. Blair was released.

June 5, 1867, John Millian was indicted by the grand jury for the murder of Julia Bulette. His trial began July 2. The jury found John Millian guilty as charged. He appealed to the Nevada Supreme Court but the verdict was upheld. February 2, 1868, Millian was sentenced to be hanged April 24, 1868.

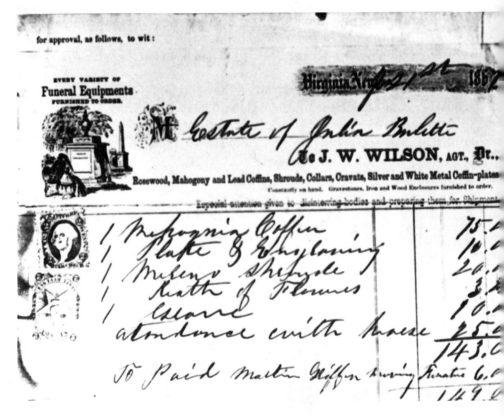

Julia Bulette's funeral bill which totaled $149. She had a mahogany coffin with an engraved plate.

Julia's unpaid liquor bill became part of her probate proceedings. This bill showed that Julia and her customers preferred wine and whiskey not champagne as legend and myth claim.

Julia's doctor bill which shows that she had seen the doctor 8 times in December before her death.

Julia Bulette's original gravesite on Flowery Hill. To make the site more visible to tourists, the grave fence was moved to a lower part of the hill. The curious and adventurous can attempt to locate Julia's real grave on Flowery Hill. Nevada Historical Society.

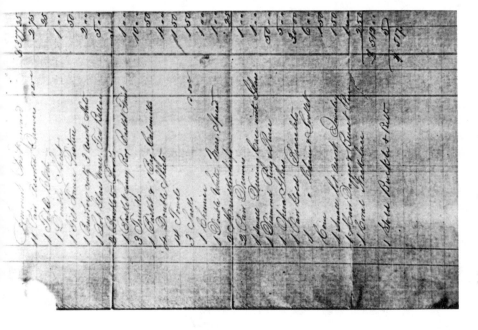

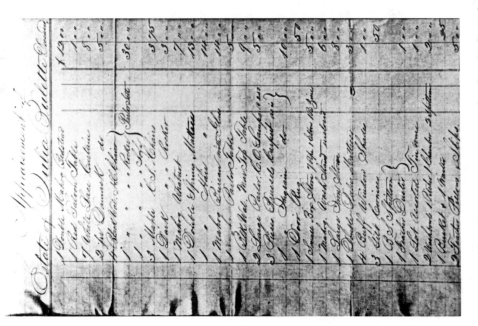

Here and on the next page is a complete list of Julia Bulette's property which was assessed for an estate sale. Her total property was assessed at a value of $517 but brought a great deal more at the estate auction.

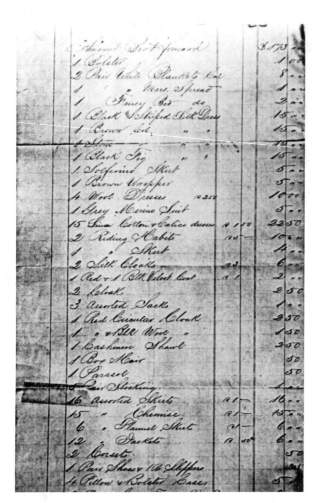

Left, last list of Julia's property. Below, the natural amphitheater one mile north of Virginia City below the Geiger Grade where Millian was likely hanged.

The Hanging of John Millian

Millian was scheduled to be hanged at noon, April 24. At 8 a.m. a crowd began to gather at the courthouse on B Street where John Millian awaited. By 10 a.m., B Street and the sidewalks swarmed with a mass of people, each hoping to catch a last glimpse of Julia Bulette's murderer. Balconies were filled; the crowd surrounded the courthouse and pushed its way into the courthouse hallway. Heads crowded about the courthouse windows.

At 11:30 Millian's carriage arrived accompanied by 30-40 Special Deputy Sheriffs with Henry rifles. Sixty National Guardsmen arrived with fixed bayonets. The Guardsmen and Sheriffs formed a line on each side of the walk from the courthouse door to the carriage. Millian shortly emerged from the courthouse accompanied by Fathers Manogue and Clarke. Millian was rushed into the carriage and the shades were drawn.

The Deputy Sheriffs and Guardsmen fought their way through the crowd for half an hour as they slowly made their way to the gallows site a little more than a mile north of town. The gallows had been erected in a ravine 150 yards below the Geiger Grade in a sort of natural amphetheater. The site was very near the Jewish cemetery.

Thousands of men, women and children, lined the carriage route along C Street. Near the gallows, Millian's carriage was parked on the Geiger Grade; then he was rushed down to the gallows. Immediately, the Sheriffs and Guardsmen formed a square surrounding the gallows. The priests, press and physicians stood in front. Nearly four thousand people watched from the Geiger Grade and the surrounding hills.

Millian quickly stepped up the gallows and gazed earnestly at the noose. Sheriff Leconey read the death warrant. Then Millian kneeled while the priests prayed for him.

Sheriff Mulcahy asked Millian if he had anything to say. Millian took from his pocket a sheet of paper and read it in French. The speech lasted about ten minutes. Millian denied killing Bulette as he had done while jailed. He thanked many of the women of Virginia City for the gifts of food they had brought him while he was in jail. He especially thanked a Mr. Hall and his family. At this point, Hall and his boys stepped up to the gallows and shook Millian's hands.

Then Millian shook the Sheriff's hands and kissed the priests. He stepped forward to the trap. A black hood was placed over his head and then the noose. At 12:42 the trap sprang open and Millian fell six feet. He was killed instantly though his heart continued beating for another thirteen minutes. After twenty-five minutes, Millian was pronounced dead and placed in his coffin. It is not known where he was buried.

The arrest, conviction and punishment of John Millian for Julia Bulette's murder was unique. Though other prostitutes and madams were murdered, their murderers were never captured and they escaped the justice of the law.

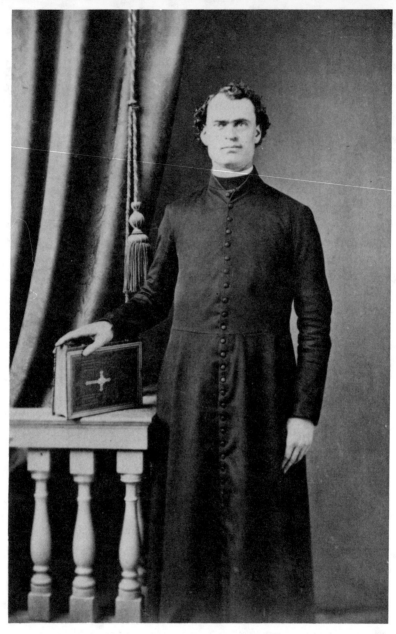

Father Manogue, the beloved. Manogue was physically quite strong as well as caring. The miners highly respected him. Manogue led funeral services for madam Jessie Lester and prayed for John Millian before he was hanged. Special Collections, University of Nevada, Reno.

Prostitution was banned in Storey County in 1947 following a Virginia City scandal involving a gun battle, the murder of a prostitute and a suicide by hanging. But in 1970, the Storey County Commissioners again legalized prostitution. Though prostitution appears inactive today in Virginia City, there are brothels located north and south of highway 50 between Virginia City and Carson City.

Charles DeLong, Millian's attorney. His only defense was that Millian must have been insane to attempt to sell Bulette's belongings. Special Collections, University of Nevada Reno.

Acknowledgements

Once again, I must thank my wife, Edie, for her support and encouragement in my writing. Edie also caught many manuscript misspellings and typeset errors.

Richard Bendix was a big help again in photographing important documents and the author's cover photo.

Phil Earl of the Nevada State Historical Society was helpful in obtaining particular historic photographs.

Bob Blesse of the Special Collections, University of Nevada, Reno, was also helpful in obtaining historic photographs.

Last, but always first, thank you Lord Jesus for showing me the way.

Here are other books on Prostitution by George Williams III. Write or call **1-800-487-6610** to order or to request a complete list of George's books. Each book is autographed and personally inscribed by George.

NEW! In the Last of the Wild West. The true story of the author's attempt to expose the murders of prostitutes and corruption in modern day Virginia City, Storey County, Nevada, home of the largest legal brothel in the United States. 272 pages. AUTOGRAPHED. $12.95 quality paperback; $27.95 hard cover. Copyright 1992.

ROSA MAY: THE SEARCH FOR A MINING CAMP LEGEND Virginia city, Carson City and Bodie, California were towns Rosa May worked as a prostitute and madam 1873-1912. Read her remarkable true story based on 3 1/2 years of research. Praised by the *Los Angeles Times* and *Las Vegas Review Journal*. Includes 30 rare photos, 26 personal letters. 240 pages. AUTOGRAPHED. $10.95 quality paperback; hard cover, $16.95. Soon to be a television movie.

THE REDLIGHT LADIES OF VIRGINIA CITY, NEVADA Virginia City was the richest mining camp in the American West. The silver from its mines built San Francisco and helped the Union win the Civil War. From 1860-95, Virginia City had one of the largest redlight districts in America. Here women from around the world worked the world's oldest profession. Author Williams tells the stories of the strange lives of the redlight girls, their legends and violent deaths. Based on newspaper accounts, county records and U.S. Census information. Perhaps the best and most informative book on prostitution in the old West. Plenty of historic photos, illustration and letters. 48 pages. AUTOGRAPHED. $5.95 quality paperback; hard cover, $10.95.

Name_____

Address_____

City_____State_____Zip_____

Please send me the following books:

__copy(ies) *In the Last of the Wild West* 12.95 pap., 27.95 hard cover
__copy(ies) *Rosa May: The Search For A Mining Camp Legend*, 9.95 pap., 16.95 hardcover
__copy(ies) *Redlight Ladies of Virginia City*, 5.95 pap., 10.95 hard cover

Please mail your order to: **Tree By The River Publishing, PO Box 935-R, Dayton, NV 89403**
Or call **Toll Free 1-800-487-6610** and order with **Visa** or **MasterCard**